Coconut™

Coco-notes

A Book of Notes
to Tear and Share

American Girl®

Questions or comments? Call 1-800-845-0005, or write
American Girl, P.O. Box 620497, Middleton, WI 53562-0497.
Visit our Web site at **americangirl.com**

Printed in China.
03 04 05 06 07 08 LEO 10 9 8 7 6 5 4 3
American Girl®, Coconut™, and the Coconut designs and logos
are trademarks of Pleasant Company.
Editorial Development: Elizabeth Chobanian, Michelle Watkins
Art Direction and Design: Camela Decaire, Chris Lorette David
Production: Kendra Pulvermacher, Mindy Rappe, Cindy Hach
Illustrations: Casey Lukatz

Send a friend a smile with a **Coco-note!**

Fill it in, tear it out, fold it up, and pass it on! Choose from
oodles of notes sprinkled with Coconut spirit! You'll find
invitations, coupons, fortune tellers, and more!
Personalize them with your own messages and seal them
with Coconut stickers. Together with Coconut, you'll be sure
to brighten up a friend's day!

Fold a Fortune

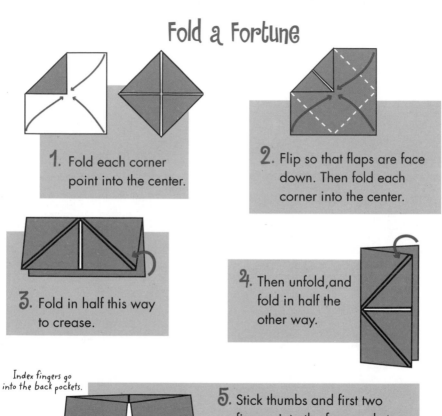

1. Fold each corner point into the center.

2. Flip so that flaps are face down. Then fold each corner into the center.

3. Fold in half this way to crease.

4. Then unfold, and fold in half the other way.

Index fingers go into the back pockets.

Thumbs go into the front pockets.

5. Stick thumbs and first two fingers into the four pockets. Push all pockets to a point to begin playing!

Let's Hang Out!

Can you come over . . .

☐ after school today?

☐ after school tomorrow?

☐ this weekend?

It would be fun to

....

....

....

To..

From..................................
(and Coconut)

fold fold fold fold

Movie Night!

Come on over

to my house this weekend for
popcorn and
your pick of any **video**.

To..

From..

(and Coconut)

Happy Birthday!

I've made three birthday wishes for you:

1. _____

   _____

2. _____

   _____

3. _____

   _____

May all your birthday wishes
—and mine—
come true!

fold

fold

fold

fold

To..

From..

(and Coconut)

You go, girl!

I'm so proud of you for

....

....

....

You are paws-itively one of a kind!

fold

fold

To..

From..

(and Coconut)

fold

fold

I'm sorry...

I feel **so bad** about

_____

_____

_____

Will you please **forgive me?**

fold

fold

To....................................

From..................................

(and Coconut)

fold

fold

Friendship is a
sheltering tree.

Samuel Taylor Coleridge

To..

From..

(and Coconut)

Psssssst!

I have a secret:

_____

_____

_____

Shh . . . don't tell a soul!
(Tear this note into tiny pieces and
throw it away when no one's looking!)

To..

From...
(and Coconut)

Me to the Rescue!

Need a helping hand?
Got a chore that's a bore?
Two can do the job better than one.

This coupon entitles you to
an afternoon of help
from yours truly!

To ....

From...........................

(and Coconut)

Thank you!

A good friend brightens your day.

It was so nice of you to _____

_____

_____

_____

_____

You're the best!

To ....

From ....

(and Coconut)

Zzzzzzzzzzzzz . . .

I had a **dream** last night. It was:

- [ ] wonderful!
- [ ] funny!
- [ ] scary!
- [ ] weird!

Here's what I remember:

_____

_____

_____

Know what it means?
If so, write below:

_____

_____

_____

To....................................

From..............................
(and Coconut)

Ooh-la-la!

You're invited to **a spa sleepover** at my house! This coupon entitles you to:

☐ a **hairstyling** (by me!)

and

☐ a **manicure!** (also by me!)

Come on over for pampering, polish, and popcorn!

To...

From..................................
(and Coconut.)

fold

fold

fold

fold

Oops!

I'm SO embarrassed! Here's what happened:

_____

_____

Any suggestions on how I can save face?
If so, write them here:

_____

_____

Blushing,_____

fold

fold

fold

fold

To.......................................

From.......................................

(and Coconut)

Dear _____,

Thank you for being my friend.

The three things I love most about you are:

1. _____

2. _____

3. _____

I will always remember

_____

_____

Friends Forever,

_____

fold

fold

fold

fold

To..

From..

(and Coconut)

S.O.S.

I need some advice.

Care to lend an ear?

Can we talk:

- ☐ at recess?
- ☐ after school?
- ☐ tonight?
- ☐ this weekend?

Hint: My problem has to do with

_____

_____

_____

fold

fold

To................................

From................................
(and Coconut)

fold

fold

Woooooooow! What a day!

I'm so:
- ❑ excited!
- ❑ nervous!
- ❑ bored!
- ❑ other _____

I'm going to ....

....

....

I'm wondering if ....

....

....

Do you think I should ....

....?

Write what you think below…

....

....

. . . and pass back to me!

To..

From..

(and Coconut.)

fold

fold

fold

fold

Let's Hang Out!

Can you come over . . .

- ☐ after school today?
- ☐ after school tomorrow?
- ☐ this weekend?

It would be fun to

....

....

....

To.....................................

From.....................................

(and Coconut)

Happy Birthday!

I've made three birthday wishes for you:

1. _____

_____

2. _____

_____

3. _____

_____

May all your birthday wishes
—and mine—
come true!

To ....

From ....

(and Coconut.)

You go, girl!

I'm so proud of you for

....

....

....

 You are paws-itively
one of a kind!

I'm sorry...

I feel **so bad** about

_____

_____

_____

Will you please **forgive me?**

To.............................

From.............................
(and Coconut)

"stay" is a charming word in a friend's vocabulary.

Louisa May Alcott

fold

fold

To..

From..

(and Coconut.)

fold

fold

Pssssssst!
I have a secret:

_____

_____

_____

Shh . . . don't tell a soul!
(Tear this note into tiny pieces and
throw it away when no one's looking!)

To.....................................

From.....................................

(and Coconut)

fold fold fold fold

Me to the Rescue!

Need a helping hand?
Got a chore that's a bore?
Two can do the job better than one.

This coupon entitles you to
an afternoon of help
from yours truly!

To..

From..
(and Coconut)

Thank you!

A good friend brightens your day.
It was so nice of you to

_____

_____

_____

_____

_____

You're the best!

To ....

From.............................
(and Coconut.)

Dear _____ ,

Thank you for being my friend.

The three things I love most about you are:

1. _____

2. _____

3. _____

I will always remember

_____

_____

Friends Forever,

_____

To..

From..

(and Coconut)

S.O.S.

I need some advice.

Care to **lend an ear?**

Can we talk:
- ☐ at recess?
- ☐ after school?
- ☐ tonight?
- ☐ this weekend?

Hint: My problem has to do with

_____

_____

_____

To...

From...

(and Coconut)

It's a Party!

You're invited!

To: _____

Where: _____

When: _____

Bring: _____

_____

RSVP by _____

Hope you can come!

To........................

From........................

(and Coconut)

fold

fold

fold

fold

It's a Party!

You're invited!

To: _____

Where: _____

When: _____

Bring: _____

_____

RSVP by _____

Hope you can come!

To.......................................

From.......................................

(and Coconut)

It's a Party!

You're invited!

To: ....

Where: ....

When: ....

Bring: ....

....

RSVP by ....

Hope you can come!

To..

From....................................

(and Coconut)

It's a Party!

You're invited!

To: ....

Where: ....

When: ....

Bring: ....

....

RSVP by ....

Hope you can come!

To....................................

From....................................

(and Coconut)

It's a Party!

You're invited!

To: ....

Where: ....

When: ....

Bring: ....

....

RSVP by ....

Hope you can come!

To..

From..

(and Coconut)

It's a Party!

You're invited!

To: ....

Where: ....

When: ....

Bring: ....

....

RSVP by ....

Hope you can come!

To...

From..

(and Coconut.)

fold

fold

fold

fold

It's a Party!

You're invited!

To: _____

Where: _____

When: _____

Bring: _____

_____

RSVP by _____

Hope you can come!

fold
fold
fold
fold

To..

From...
(and Coconut)